Single Mamas

Group Leaders Guide

INTRODUCTION

Leaders Guide — For Starting a Single Mamas Group

This guide is designed to help women who desire to begin a group for single mamas in their community. You may be going through a church, community center, or group home. Whatever your home base may be, this guide is a step-by-step help towards starting a group with a strong foundation. Excitement, enthusiasm, and passion are wonderful, but without a strategic plan, even the best vision can fail.

You may be married, a couple, or a single mama yourself. But what matters is your heart to help single mamas become strong, self-confident women and parents.

As you read through these pages, keep in mind all groups are different. Demographics, culture, ethnicity all play a part in the group you are planning. Group dynamics and structures may vary, but the mutual need for wisdom, resources, encouragement and friendship are the fuel for single mama groups.

Remember, there are many single moms who have weathered this storm, regained their confidence, let go of their past, and brought balance to their life again. These women are being equipped to help other single mamas going through their various stages of parenting and life traumas. If you are reading this, I believe YOU are one of them! Just be prepared before you launch into your ministry.

Don't lose confidence if things don't goes as planned in the beginning, there will always be missteps. Just keep focused on your goals, your team, and your single mamas!
I believe in you! I know you can do this!

Chapters

Chapter 1

Becoming a Leader

I can do all things through Christ who gives me strength.
  — Philippians 4:13 (NIV)

Becoming a Leader

Do you want to start a group, but aren't sure if you're ready or able? Do you feel your own past or current struggles eliminate you as leader material? Well, you've got the first best ingredient of a single mama leader—passion to help other moms! Below are a few indicators to help you know if you're ready to lead others. Confidence comes with experience, so give yourself a chance to grow.

To know if you're personally ready to begin a Single Mama group, whether you're a single mom, a married woman, or a couple, go through the checklist below. You don't have to be a perfect person or even totally healed from your past, but mama's will be looking to you for hope, guidance, leadership, and strength. You will want to be prepared yourself.

Ready to lead characteristics

You've moved beyond your own personal loss, abuse, or abandonment. You may not be in a perfect world, but you are not stuck in your issues.

You can avoid speaking negative words regarding your ex.

You can teach lessons from the past, without sharing bitterness.

You are free from controlling, destructive, or addictive behaviors (Alcohol, drugs, cutting, eating disorders, abuse).

Your home is not in chaos (not perfect, but not in constant chaos or drama).

You have a mentor you continue to learn from (someone who encourages and stands with you).

You have faith that God can heal and restore lives.

You have a personal testimony of your own journey of healing or restoration.

You have a desire to lead others to a better place, and help them become a better parent and confident individual.

You have a humble, not superior attitude.

You possess empathy (understanding) – but not enabling/coddling behaviors.

<u>You may not be ready to lead at this time</u>

You feel all (or almost all) men are untrustworthy, or bad.

You have a defeated attitude about most things—evidenced by depression, a victim mentality, or negative expressions in your words or attitudes.

You feel the world is against you, single moms, or women in general.

Children in your home are disrespectful, defiant, or abusive. (Children are a priority, requiring your time and attention. It will be hard to focus on leadership if your family is still dealing with major issues.)

Note: Not at this time doesn't mean never! Continue to heal, grow, learn, and prepare for your time to lead!

Chapter 2

Defining Your Purpose

&

Setting Your Goals

And the Lord answered me: "Write the vision; make it plain on tablets, so he may run who reads it. —Habakkuk 2:2 (NLT)

Defining your Purpose, Setting your Goals

In order to begin a small group, your first step is to establish your purpose and goals for this group.

Define your purpose and goals. Write them out!

This should be a brief paragraph that outlines your purpose and goals as a single mama group.

Here is an example:

> This (name of your group) group has been established as a safe place for single mamas to gather and find relief from the pressures of single parenting. Our goal is to work together as a team to strengthen our faith, gain wisdom, enhance our parenting skills, encourage and resource one-another, and find hope for a better future.

Format of your Group

Determine if your group will focus on (a) discipleship (faith building), (b) social activities, (c) encouragement through discussions, (d) all of these? Many groups encompass all three aspects.

Discipleship

Decide which directed study methods you will use.

The Bible, topical studies, resource books, DVDs.

Plan topics for your first quarter of meetings.

Suggested topics to start your own brainstorming:

Discover who God is and how He views you.

Overcoming fears.

How a relationship with God changes your outlook.

Importance of Forgiveness – letting go of your past (and the controlling people in your life).

Getting 'unstuck' (emotionally and physically).

<u>Social Activities</u> —Outings with other Single Moms

How often do you want outings?

Will they be spontaneous or planned, or both?

Who will lead or organize activities?

If spontaneous, can this come from within the group?

What are the leaders responsibilities?

How will costs be met (individually, donations, etc)

<u>Encouragement</u>

Sources of encouragement include:

> Shared stories from within the group

> Guest speakers

> Books or DVD's

> Worship: regularly, occasionally, special worship leader presentation on the power of worship.

Limit negative vocabulary within the group (moms can be real and honest, but don't allow negativity to rule the group.)

Structure of the Group

Will you be following a book or DVD?

Will it be conversationally led (no formal teaching)?

Will it be leader led with question and answer times?

Will your group work together to find answers to issues?

Will there be breakouts, whole group discussions, or both?

What helps or resources can you offer the group? (Websites, books, articles, podcasts, or testimonies.)

Will you have a Facebook group? If so, what's its purpose?

> Discussions? Encouraging words? Event planning?

> Who will be the administrator(s)?

> Private or open group? I suggest private to protect moms.

Is this a Community outreach or local church group only?

Will you invite and welcome neighbors or friends?

Are non-believers to be included and welcomed?

If so, plan your strategy to invite those outside your church cirlce. Use vocabulary non-believers will understand.

Suggested places to promote your group: (Always seek permission from owners or managers.)

Apartments, daycare centers, laundromats, after-school care, radio ads (ads are often donated for this cause).

Naming Your Group

Choose a name that fits your goals and group dynamic.

Look online for duplicate names in your area or on FB so you don't duplicate them and cause confusion.

Make sure initials for your group don't have meanings you don't desire.

Local Support

Your local church or community support is vital for:

Prayer support — for leaders & mamas.

Volunteers — to cut costs for childcare workers.

Donations — help pay for advertising, kids crafts, snacks, room rentals (if not hosted in a church).

Building community awareness and relationship.

Establish Group Meeting Rules

Meeting rules will help minimize problems down the road. Rules may include some of the following:

Respect privacy—what is shared in the meeting, stays in the meeting.

Respect each-others opinion and voice.

Respect each-others story.

Respect the home/meeting place—clean up after your meeting.

Respect start and end times—to show consideration for the host site, child care workers, and everyone's schedules. Mama's coming late can still join, but they should not hold up or disrupt the meeting.

Respect the child care provided—do not bring sick children to the meeting.

These are just suggestions; you may have other thoughts to add to your list. However, if rules are established in the beginning, it makes it easier to address problems that may arise.

Note: By writing out your purpose and goals, defining your audience, planning your discussion topics, and establishing group rules, you're on a solid road to grow your group and accomplish the purpose you desire.

Chapter 3

Selecting Your Team

Plans go wrong for lack of advice; many advisers bring success.
— Proverbs 15:22 (NLT)

Selecting Your Team

Don't go it alone! You will become overwhelmed and burned out without at least one assistant/partner on your team.

Selecting and Establishing Your Team

Team size and responsibilities

The number of assistants will often depend on the size of your group or pool of potential single moms.

Minimum: 2 or 3 team leaders (including you)

Share responsibilities with your team

Teaching/leading (after they've been trained)

Providing snacks

Taking calls/questions from SM's

Discuss teaching options, group issues, direction, searches for local resources available to mamas, etc.

Recruitment & Protection

Require background checks on all leaders (they will be in contact with the children as well). Since churches run background checks on children's workers, your pastoral staff can give you the required links for your volunteers.

Consider requiring a free online 'giftings' assessment. These evaluations help you place volunteers in positions where they'll flourish. You'll need creative thinkers, organizers, and compassionate leaders. Free assessment testing sites include:

https://discpersonalitytesting.com/free-disc-test/

https://www.truity.com/test/type-finder-person-ality-test-new

Choose people who are in good standing with the church leadership, or in your community. You want your group to have a good, trustworthy reputation!

Avoid contentious or argumentative people on your team.

Choose those with a good reputation in other volunteer or supervisory positions.

Choose reliable and cooperative persons.

Seek leaders who know their boundaries. (See the below *All Team Leaders* section for guidance)

<u>Diverse backgrounds are welcome</u>

Single Mom leaders

Choose those with healthy attitudes: No bitter attitudes towards exes, men in general, or the world.

Choose moms who have recovered or are stabilized from their own trauma.

Couple leaders

Don't eliminate the idea of a couple being part of the team. (You may even be a couple desiring to start a group yourself.) A couple can offer wise counsel from their years of life and parenting experiences. However, there are precautions you must take, whenever a man is participating. Single moms can interpret kindness from a man as affection. There must be no one-on-one help or interaction for the protection of both the moms and the man. That being said, a mature couple can have a lot to offer a Single Mama group.

Married women

You don't have to be a single mom to have a heart for her needs, or wisdom for her issues. Know the motivation, the history, and experience of any leader you choose to be part of your team. (I know married women who have started and continue to lead successful single mom groups.)

<u>All Team Leaders</u>

Should exhibit the following traits or are growing in these areas. *

Empathy towards single moms (not judgmental).

Have mentoring/discipleship skills (this will grow with experience).

Can set safe boundaries for themselves and the moms. (A balance of care and help, without being pulled into their drama, or enable any harmful habits.)

Display spiritual and emotional growth and stability.

They are teachable (not stubborn or rebellious – or have a need to always be right).

They are team players (they can follow your vision).

They are kind (they may have strong personalities, but they exhibit compassion).

They are able to stabilize their own family, finances, and employment (they may be working on these areas, but you recognize their growth).

They display attitudes of joy, patience and forgiveness.

They are shown to be rational in their reactions when under stress.

They possess listening skills – not just directors (bossy).

They understand the power of forgiveness and being set free from controlling reactions.

* Volunteers will not be perfect, however, they should show character qualities that will benefit the single mamas and the group as a whole.

Chapter 4

Leading Tips & Guides

I will instruct you and teach you in the way you should go; I will counsel you with my loving eye on you. —Psalm 32:8 (NIV)

Leader Training

Leading Tips & Guides

Consider yourself and your team as 'guides'. Those who offer paths, maps, and choices to others.

Leading Goals for Your Team

To act as guides to a stronger faith, better lifestyle, improved parenting skills, and better reactions.

To offer new life choices, not attempt to 'change' mamas (that's God's role), or make choices for them.

To love mamas without becoming entangled in their situation.

To give suggestions and resources, while understanding it's not a leader's job to 'fix' the moms or their kids.

Don't Give Up Quickly, Change Takes Time

If a mama take a wrong turn, offer her *grace* and a re-start.

> If they choose dangerous paths, offer them resources to get back on track.

> You are offering guidance, opportunities, resources, but you are not responsible for their ultimate choices.

Celebrate the victories! No matter how small they may seem to you, they are huge wins for the moms.

Always encourage! Remain upbeat, calm, and the leader (don't fall into their world, but lead them towards a better one).

Remember, you cannot control their lives; you control only the way you lead or mentor them.

Maintaining Conversational Flow

Leaders must maintain the flow and feel of a meeting. You

cannot allow one person (even a leader) to dominate conversations. I've seen leaders take over the group with their strong opinions or personalities. If this happens, first address the person privately one-on-one. If they continue to dominate or try to control the flow, address it as it happens during the meeting. If you must, cut in (nicely), to get the discussion back on track or to allow others in the group to speak. This is never easy, but it must be done, or *timid moms will just quit coming.* (Whether it's a leader or a mama who has become the problem, address it quickly—problems left unresolved only grow). If a leader is unable to allow other leaders or moms to speak or have input, they should be asked to step down from leadership. (They may be open to some personal counseling if this is an ongoing issue for them.)

Having a list of rules may avoid, or help resolve, some of those issues. (See Group Rules discussed on pages 14-15)

Decision Guidance

Because single moms are often overwhelmed financially, emotionally, and with child issues – sound decision making skills can become difficult. Here are a few guidelines to help train your leaders in this area.

Leaders should guide or suggest, but allow single moms to make final decisions. This builds confidence and independent thinking. Moms will reap the effects of their decisions, so they must ultimately take responsibility for them.

Offer resources (people, websites, articles) to help mamas make decisions on the following. Look for professionals within your church or community who are willing to advise moms in these specific areas:

Apartment rentals

Car purchases

House rentals or purchases

Personal, child, or teen counseling help

Financial resources or advisors

Parenting mentors or counselors

Parenting books, podcasts, or website resources

Leaders should not feel they must have answers for every question or decision. A good leader will offer direction, moral support, and encouragement in the mama's process.

Develop Trust

It's hard for single moms to extend trust. Most have gone through horrendous betrayals by their most intimate partner. Understanding this, may help your leaders be more patient and careful in building trust within your group.

Trust is hard to establish after betrayals

Be patient – let them talk when they're ready.

Be patient – allow them time to heal.

Teach them to recognize traits in others that are healthy— ie: responsibility, honesty, and a good reputation.

Remember: they may have been with someone who originally displayed those qualities, and they were still abandoned, abused, or betrayed by them. (Thus, the trust wall was built.)

Trust cannot be rushed—it can only be earned

Do not discuss their issues or confidences with anyone else —including the church prayer chain (without their permission).

Only share with the pastor or Board of Directors on issues of suicidal tendencies, child abuse concerns, or for counseling references.

Don't judge their actions—their backstory explains much of their behavior.

Avoid showing 'shock' at their stories. Just listen. You

don't need answers for their story, just be a listening ear.

Redirect Emotions

Teach moms *positive outlets* for their hurts and frustrations, rather than allow them to wallow or constantly repeat their story. Positive healing outlets could include the following:

Learning to forgive themselves and others, for *their sake.*

Volunteering to help others, thus taking their sole focus of life off themselves.

Writing something good that happened in their day—no matter how small it may seem.

Turning their focus to the future, possibilities, and dreams instead of their past. Most have lost the ability to dream or hope for anything different than their rather dismal current situation.

Avoid saying "it's time to move on". Everyone has their own timetable. Trust, healthy friendships, and boundaries will all help them heal and move on.

Setting Boundaries

Some single mamas can drain even the most enthusiastic leader. Your team may be made up of compassionate and caring people, but without boundaries, they can burn out quickly. Learning to set boundaries not only helps leaders, it helps moms become stronger, independent, and more responsible women and parents.

Train leaders how to limit phone conversations

This becomes necessary for those mamas who are very 'needy' (wanting leaders to solve their problems, while not taking steps of their own).

Set time frames for both frequency and length of calls. Balance compassion with wisdom.

Unless there is an emergency do not allow moms to *dominate* your personal or family time with calls or constant interruptions regarding their problems—this deepens dependency. Be a friend available to talk, but do not allow invasive, unhealthy behaviors.

Continuous calls on the same subject must come to an end. Let them know you'll continue conversations when they've taken one step towards improving it themselves (counseling may be their next step). Remind them of the specific first step they need to take towards their goal. This encourages initiative and responsibility for their own family and life.

Have counseling recommendations available for moms in need of therapy. You can get references from your pastor, local social services, or women's shelters.

Boundaries with the children are vital

Leaders can get emotionally involved with the children. Leaders must learn not encroach on the role of the single mom over her children (overriding mom's choices, getting too emotionally attached to the children, or in other ways threaten the mother's role with her children).

Always protect the children

If abuse is reported, suspected, or obvious —you must report it immediately!

Have child/youth counselor resources available for moms whose children are in need of more professional help.

One-on-one Mentoring Guides

Mentors guide moms towards independent thinking and choices, not a dependency upon them.

Mentoring is often just friendship – not an official 'task'. They will watch your behaviors and reactions to learn new ones. They may ask for advice, but should not be 'told' what to do.

Mentoring guides and questions to be asked:

Why do they want a mentor? Are you the right person for that goal? If not, who could be the right person for them?

What specific behaviors does the mama want to change or improve?

Offer steps to begin their journey to change. This could include reading a book, listening to some podcasts or DVD's, meeting with someone who has overcome the same issues, etc.

Follow-up: Did they read the book, listen to the podcast, etc, and what did they get out of it for themselves? What first step have they taken towards their goal?

Seek discernment to recognize manipulation/self-pity.

These behaviors are roadblocks to growth or change, and take advantage of a caring leader.

Leaders must protect their time and personal involvement when a mama wants to drain them, without making any effort to change herself (take any steps towards progress). You are not required to take repeated calls on the same issue if a mama is making _no_ effort of her own.

After repeated failures to achieve even a simple goal, (or no attempts towards a goal), put your mentoring on hold. Ask them to call or see you again, when they've taken a first step towards their agreed upon goal.

Do not take blame or responsibility for their failures— poor choices, decisions, or staying in a victim mode.

Know when to let go of those who do not want to change (God will let you know when it's time). You can always begin again at a later date if their attitude or commitment level changes.

Remember you are not a professional counselor!

Learn to recognize when a mom needs professional counseling and have a list of local counselors (within her budget) available as a resource for her.

Chapter 5

Recognizing & Resolving

Harmful Behaviors

For God is not a God of disorder but of peace, as in all the meetings of God's holy people. —I Corinthians 14:33 (NLT)

Recognizing & Resolving
Harmful Behaviors

Train your leaders to recognize, remain calm, and handle unhealthy traits of agression or control. (The list of group rules you established earlier helps defer many issues.)

Actions or Attitudes Not Acceptable in the Group

Constant outbursts of anger.

Belittling others in the group (showing disrespect).

Domineering group discussions.

Substance abuse (learn the signs and symptoms of drug/alcohol abuse at www.mayoclinic).

Resolution Options

Talk individually with the mom, explain the problem, discuss ways to remedy the issue.

If a mom has a combative personality, have a co-leader or staff person with you when addressing the issue. This would be a rare situation, as most moms in a group are looking for help, guidance, and community. However, there are those rare individuals who do not want help, only a place to vent or control.

Is she open to counseling? (Offer resources)

Temporary removal from the group may be necessary.

Let her know she is loved, but you've established rules to protect all the moms, and the group, from unhealthy situations.

Remind her that personal growth and healing will not occur if she *constantly* vents, blames others, stays in her past, or clings to a victim mentality.

Addressing Dating and Relationship Issues

If a mama has a 'bad' relationship history, encourage her to avoid dating until she's reached a place of restoration within their own life and family.

Children must also be ready for their mom to date. When children have experienced loss and instability, they have little trust, and lots of fears—they are very vulnerable. If her children are resisting her dating, she would be wise to forgo dating until the children are ready or even grown. (This may be hard, but she does not want to make a choice between her child and a man.)

Remember: You are not their mother or their decision maker. but you can offer sound, healthy suggestions.

Cautions

Bringing any 'unknown' or unreliable person into their family life can cause more instability, fears, or stress.

It can also become a dangerous situation for their kids.

Dating should not be her emotional outlet without care and boundaries to protect herself and her children.

Loneliness

Loneliness is real and has a huge impact on single moms. However, they will not have the same drive to date (have sex), when they learn a few simple ways to overcome their loneliness.

Redirect thoughts—movies they watch or books they read.

Set new personal goals that will make them feel better about themselves. (Career change, hobbies, volunteering, educational advancement, etc.)

Call friends when they are in an emotional slump to avoid thoughts or the need to 'find a guy'.

Developing healthy friendships is vital, and a Single

Mama group is a great place to start new friendships.

As mama's learn of God's love for them and trust is built, they learn to turn to God, not a man for their emotional support.

Teach them how to share these same principals with their children and teens through honest discussions, studying scriptures on God's Promises, and learning God's plans for their life and future.

God is the defender of widows (abandoned) and a father to the fatherless (Psalm 68:5).

Moms who date on-line

Encourage moms to date locally. They must be able to meet the real friends and family of the person they're dating; people who can vouch for their temperament, and history. People can be whomever they create on-line without someone to validate them. Long distance dating can be a very dangerous situation for moms & their children.

It's not wise to travel or move your family for an online dating relationship (I've seen moms do this).

Successful online dates (marriages) have come from local dates, with local friends (on both sides). They've had the same faith and family goals, solid job histories, and both parties were in an emotionally stable time of life.

Chapter 6

Restoring Self-Esteem

For I know the plans I have for you," says the Lord. "They are plans for good and not for disaster, to give you a future and a hope." —Jeremiah 29:11 (NLT)

Leader Training

Restoring Self-esteem

Most single moms have been demeaned and left with a feeling of worthlessness. They believe it's *their* flaws that have caused their problems, see themselves as ugly or un-desirable, feel hopeless, and are without vision for a future (especially a happy one). Many of these thoughts and feelings come from words spoken to them over a long period of time. Many generational single moms expect poor treatment or have feelings of defeat.

Suicidal Thoughts

These feelings are often directly related to low self-esteem and feelings of worthlessness.

Many single moms struggle with suicidal thoughts as their only way out of their loneliness, lack of a loving relationship, overwhelming responsibilities, and a dismal looking future. They are constantly pouring out their strength and emotions to their kids and their job, but are never replenished.

However, these suicidal thoughts can flee when there is a place for moms to feel refreshed (at the feet of Jesus and in a Single Mama group). When they believe God loves them, and begin to feel good about who they are—their desire for life, ambitions, and attitudes change.

Women who have their self-esteem restored, see themselves differently, love differently, and live differently; they have hope and seek life!

Leaders Can Build Confidence in Simple ways

Speak kind words —encouragements, compliments, and affirm their positive character traits.

Give gift cards for haircuts, or make-up appointments.

A fresh haircut, lotions, or makeup products help moms see themselves differently, and it boosts confidence.

Consider a mini spa day.

Recruit volunteers to give haircuts, massages, do nails.

Have new or slightly used clothes available for them to choose from—these often help moms gain job interviews and renews interest in their appearance again.

Offer hand massages—a good way to pray them as well.

Have giveaways—groceries, gas, and other useful gift cards.

When a person feels valued, they make better decisions for themselves and for their family.

Overcoming Shame or Guilt

Self-esteem grows with confidence, while a lack of self-esteem is often attached to feelings of shame or guilt (deserved or not). Here are a few suggestions to help moms overcome guilt or shame.

Don't judge

You have no idea how or why they ended up in their situation, and it doesn't matter! How they can overcome their past should be your focus.

Don't set time limits on grieving. Everyone grieves differently—it's shaming to set time limits.

Highlight their positives, so they will listen to new advice on changing the negatives. Criticizing their life, or parenting methods only deepens feelings of shame or worthlessness.

Teach lessons on God's love, and how God views them

Help them learn they are God's children, dearly loved, treasured, designed with a plan and a future.

Mistakes may have consequences, but God always desires to restore those who come to Him. He is the God of love and restoration! Remind them, nothing can separate them from God's love (Romans 8:35-39)

When anyone feels and believes they are loved, it changes everything! Attitudes and actions follow our level of confidence and self-esteem.

<u>Teach Lessons on forgiveness</u>

Forgiveness has no limits, and it is available for each woman regardless of her past.

Forgiveness of others, helps set moms free from the control of those who may still try to bombard her with shaming and destrutive words.

Many single moms hate themselves, taking on guilt and condemnation whether deserved or not. They need to learn to forgive themselves as well.

<u>God's love restores self-esteem</u>

When a woman feels loved (by God) regardless of her past, it changes her entire outlook on life and her self-esteem. If God can love her, she can learn to love herself. When she loves herself, she loves others in a more healthy manner. Outburst of anger diminish, walls around her heart come down, trust is restored, and her joy becomes evident.

Healthy self-esteem forms vision for a better life, better parenting, and a better future!

Chapter 7

Helping the Children

See that you do not despise one of these little ones. For I tell you that their angels in heaven, are always in the presence of my Father in heaven. —Matthew 18:10 (NIV)

Helping the Children

Each circumstance is different. However, keep in mind, many children act out because they are grieving. When a divorce or death is recent, they are grieving the loss of a parent and lifestyle. They become fearful of their future, angry at their circumstance, and are too young to know how to process these life changes. So often, they become angry, mean, mouthy, or rebellious. Some withdraw and become isolated. Try understanding their grief to better understand their reactions to life and other people. Walls of defense don't look pretty, but it may be all they know.

As you start a single mama group, children will come with it. You are not a counseling service, or a church (though you may be a para-church ministry). If you see children struggling, try speaking with the mom about options to help them overcome their anger or grief.

Helpful Reminders for Working with the Children

Building their trust is the first step. Remember to watch your words, and use discretion with every child. Talking to others about any of their issues will be a betrayal hard to rectify!

If you can get them involved in a kids church or youth group, there will often be a pastor over that area who can better minister to the children.

These following suggestions are for leaders, child-care volunteers and the mamas.

Be patient—Children may need a lot of proof you are trustworthy.

Be patient—They may need a lot of proof you will not hurt them (emotionally or physically, depending on where they've come from).

Be patient—Allow them to see healthy relationships, healthy friendships, healthy families, healthy love.

Be patient—Don't be quick to remove a child from a class. They may be acting out so they will be expelled just to avoid platitudes, correction, more change, or help—thus confirming their feelings of worthlessness or rejection.

Be firm—but loving. Always discipline in kindness, not anger.

Offer family counseling— with qualified counselors.

Provide opportunities for outings and fun gatherings— they need joy restored.

Befriend the teens—Provide encouraging books, podcasts, studies, worship streaming apps, or CD's. Connect them with a good youth group.

There may be grandparent mentors willing to pray and or interact with the children.

Screen anyone in contact with children or youth!

Chapter 8

Pre-Startup Group Preparation

So do not fear, for I am with you; do not be dismayed, for I am your God. I will strengthen you and help you; I will uphold you with my righteous right hand.
 — Isaiah 41:10 (NIV)

Pre-Startup Group Preparation

There are several final steps to take before you start your group. Carefully consider the following before advertising or launching a new group.

How often will you meet?

Weekly, bi-weekly, monthly—

> My advice is weekly whenever possible. Bi-weekly can become confusing. Monthly is too long, and it's too easy for moms to lose interest, forget, or find other activities in its place.

Choosing your meeting location

Is there a cost for the space? If so, how will you pay for this?

Is there adequate space for both the mamas and child care? *Child care must be provided for a single mom group to succeed.*

Child Care Prerequisties

Space, and any costs involved.

How many children can you properly care for?

What ages will you provide care for?

How many care providers will be needed?

How will you recruit child care providers?

From within the group or outside the group?

Volunteers vs paid?

Learning and Activity goals:

Lessons, crafts, or DVDs?

Who will pay for craft supplies or snacks if needed?

Parents, sponsored group, or through donations?

Casting Vision

You will need either your church or Community Center approval to meet in their facilities. I suggest the following to be included in your vision presentation:

Present single mom statistics for your community— found on the 2020 census.gov website

Present your **Purpose and Goals** (Chapter 2)

Present the single mom needs of your community *and* how your group can meet some of those needs.

Why, or how, their location will help meet other needs of single moms and their children. Ie: Connections to their youth and children's programs, women's or other small groups, Sunday services, or the community at large.

Present your **format** on how your group would function in their facility (Chapter 2).

Present any costs required—child care/crafts/rental fees.

> Ask if the church would be willing to cover any or all of those needs, or if the group would need to raise the funds.

Present possible team members.

> Have at least 1-2 assistant leaders on board before presenting vision to the pastor, Board, or a director.

Present a timeline.

> Discuss when the group could begin—what are the benefits of that start date, does it fit their schedule?

> How often your group will meet.

> How much space or number of rooms are needed.

> How long will each session or study normally be (weeks/months)?

Present your first suggested study – and why that book or topic?

Ask what their Church concerns might be

Ask how you can work with the church

Studies to be used (does the church require their study plan for all small groups?)

Times or days to meet (same as other church small groups?)

Do you need to be under a department head?

What would their role be in your group?

Can you present the vision to the church body or Board?

Can you solicit financial support or volunteers from the congregation?

If you're not meeting at a church

Is there a facility rental cost (how will you meet this cost?)

What are the restrictions of the building?

What are the concerns of the building Director?

How can you work to resolve those issues?

Is there space for the children (various ages)?

Are you meeting in a home? Same home or will it be alternating homes?

Is there sufficient parking for the single moms?

Will the neighborhood tolerate a weekly meeting with cars in front of their homes? (Always keep a non-hostile environment for moms and kids)

Is there a gate or passcode needed for a community building, or home meeting? Can you give that code out to a group of people?

Communicate with your team

Keep them in the loop on discussions with leadership on when you can start your group, where you'll be meeting, and any building concerns.

Know your state and local community resources

Be prepared to offer practical and emergency resources to your group.

Research and gather a current list of community and state resources for single moms—include food shelves, educational helps, specific counseling, legal aid services, and shelters for abused women.

Include government assistance websites for those just beginning the process of becoming a single mom.[1]

---

1 www.singlemamas.org – resource page

Chapter 9

First Meeting Suggestions

Therefore, my dear brothers and sisters, stand firm. Let nothing move you. Always give yourselves fully to the work of the Lord, because you know that your labor in the Lord is not in vain.
    —1 Corinthians 15:58 (NIV)

First Meeting Suggestions

Make all mamas feel welcome!

This is a new experience for many mamas, feeling anxious is a normal reaction to meeting new people, especially if they are coming to a new place (church). Do whatever you can to make them feel comfortable and accepted.

Have volunteers help mamas escort their children to their classrooms or childcare room.

If you are meeting at a church prepare the youth pastor and children's pastor that there will be new (also anxious) children needing to feel welcomed.

Supply name tags for everyone.

If you're able, prepare a meal for the families before the meeting starts as a welcome. They'll be together to begin with, then you can escort kids to their rooms. If this is not possible, offer snacks and beverages to welcome the moms.

Introduce yourself and your team

Be <u>brief</u> in all your introductions, you want to keep the moms engaged—you can lose them if you talk too much or give too much information on your first meeting. Keep it relaxed and natural.

Give a *brief* testimony—so they know you understand their situation.

Have a quick fun ice-breaker (something that will help introduce moms to each other if possible).

If the group is small, ask each mom to share their first name, how many kids they have and their ages. If the group is too large and it would take too much time do a fun overview of the group by:

Ask moms to stand who have grown kids (they'll come too), high schoolers, middle schoolers, elementary, pre-schoolers, and infants or toddlers. This will give you, and the group, an overview of moms attending.

Give a *brief* outline of the topic or study for the class, and why you chose it.

If at all possible, pre-purchase books from money raised outside of the group, especially as you launch the group. You can prepare moms to purchase books for future studies, but begin your first meeting without asking for money whenever possible.

Depending on your time, give a devotional that will peek their interest for your chosen study. Or, if available, share the overview or introduction provided in your DVD or book.

ALWAYS end on time (child care workers matter)!

If moms want to talk to you after, or request prayer, be sure they pick up their children in a timely manner.

Your first meeting should be welcoming, relaxing, engaging, and something they'd like to return to the following week.

Some single mama groups start early to offer a meal before the meeting start time every week. This may be something that works for you, or can be an occasional offering, or not done at all—however, snacks are always nice and welcome.

It's always good to have a fun kick-off event to launch your group. It may be a breakfast, lunch, dinner or other special event. Always have your followup activity or Group launch information available at that event. The followup launch should be within the month, so they don't lose interest.

Chapter 10

Passing the Leadership Torch

You have heard me teach things that have been confirmed by many reliable witnesses. Now teach these truths to other trustworthy people who will be able to pass them on to others.
     —2 Timothy 2:2 (NLT)

Continuously look for moms to mentor into leadership roles. This will grow your team, add creative ideas, and provide a means to multiply the group.

Review the *Selecting Your Team* chapter of this guide for the characteristics to look for in choosing new leaders.

Many single moms lack confidence. Some are very timid while others can be very outspoken. Your wise coaching skills will help each personality succeed (remember, the free assessment test options mentioned on page 17.)

Become a trusted guide or coach

Gradually mentor new prospects.

Learn their strengths, then encourage them in their strengths—build their confidence.

Offer resources to develop their strengths.

 Books, articles, podcasts

Listen to their concerns.

Guide them in ways to overcome or face their concerns.

Are their concerns real, or unfounded worries (single moms have many fears and anxieties. Some are based on real life situations, many are 'what if' fears.)

Real concerns need to be addressed. They may just need 'cheerleaders' to boost their confidence, or they may need personal, family or financial counseling.

Remember: You are not a counselor; you are a caring mentor. Mentors coach and lead by example and experience. Counselors have training and credentials to counsel.

Gradually give them responsibilities that fit their current strengths. Responsibilities can expand as their confidence is built. You want them to succeed from the start, not be given a job that sets them up for failure.

Start with simple tasks and build to greater ones, offer steps to successful leadership:

Schedule child care, snack rotation, other simple tasks.

Coach them in outlining a teaching session.

Show them how to research answers, find data, or gather background for a lesson.

Prepare them to teach a small portion of a session.

Do not try to put them in a leadership position too early or one that does not fit their gifting. If they feel they've failed they may quit and never try again.

Always try to duplicate yourself so the group can grow or expand through multiplication.

Your leaders may move, but they can take their knowledge with them to begin a ministry in another city or state.

Do not feel, or fear, competition with those you train. If you have someone who surpasses your abilities, feel blessed! It means you've done a good job mentoring. They will use those abilities in many areas of their life beyond your group!

Summary

Don't copy the behavior and customs of this world, but let God transform you into a new person by changing the way you think. Then you will learn to know God's will for you, which is good and pleasing and perfect.
—Romans 12:2 (NLT)

Summary

Starting anything new is scary. Being a leader can be intimidating. But if you have the heart, and a desire that doesn't seem to go away – I say go for it! You will make mistakes, but the more prepared you are the fewer mistakes will be made. Single moms are desperately looking for help, mentors, educational training, parenting tips, and friendship. *You could be the answer to their prayer!*

Do your research, plan your goals, build your team, prepare a place, and begin your group. Every group will look different, every leader will be different based on their talents and personality. But every group can offer what is most needed in their community – a Single Mamas group and *hope in Jesus Christ*.